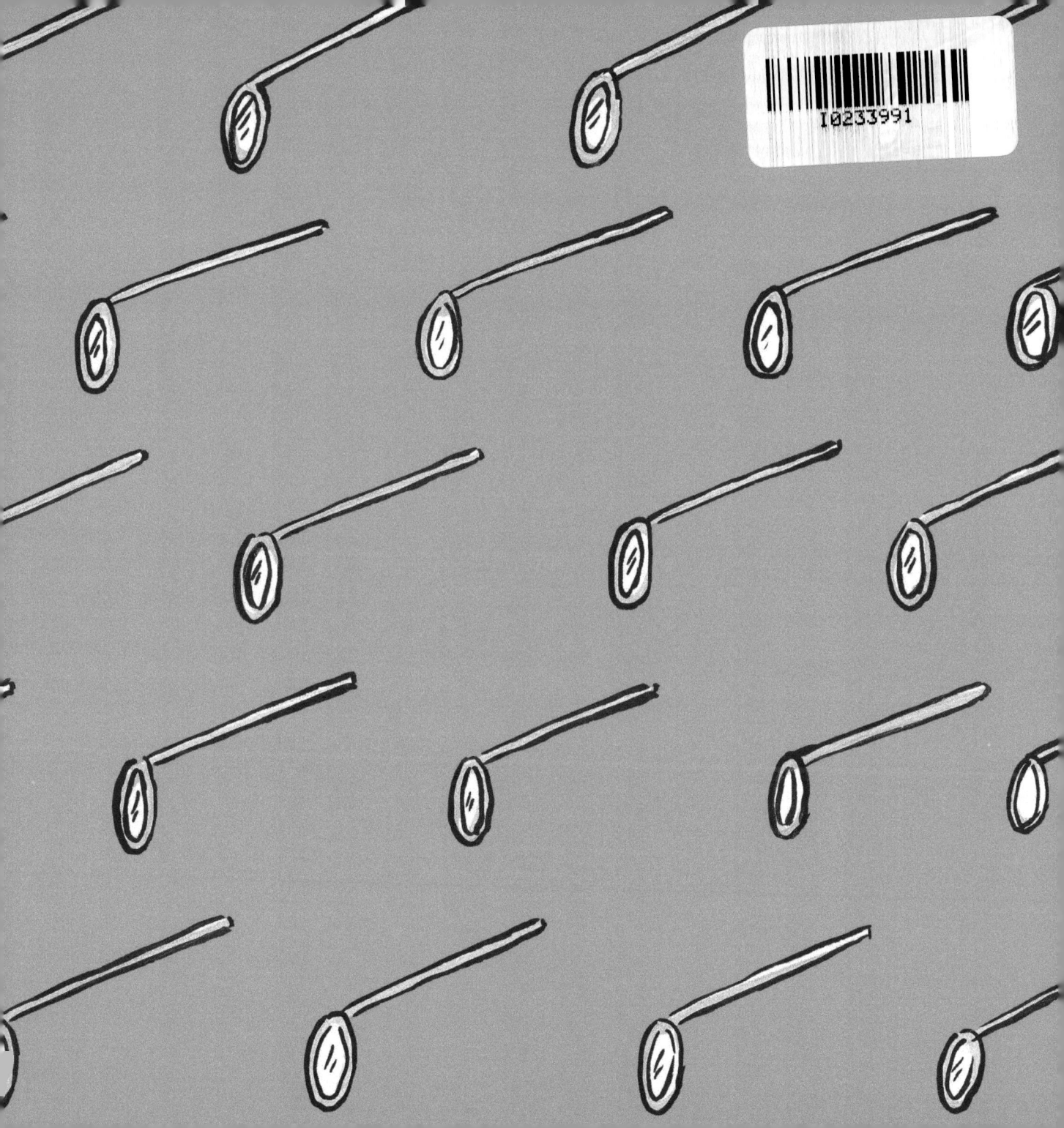

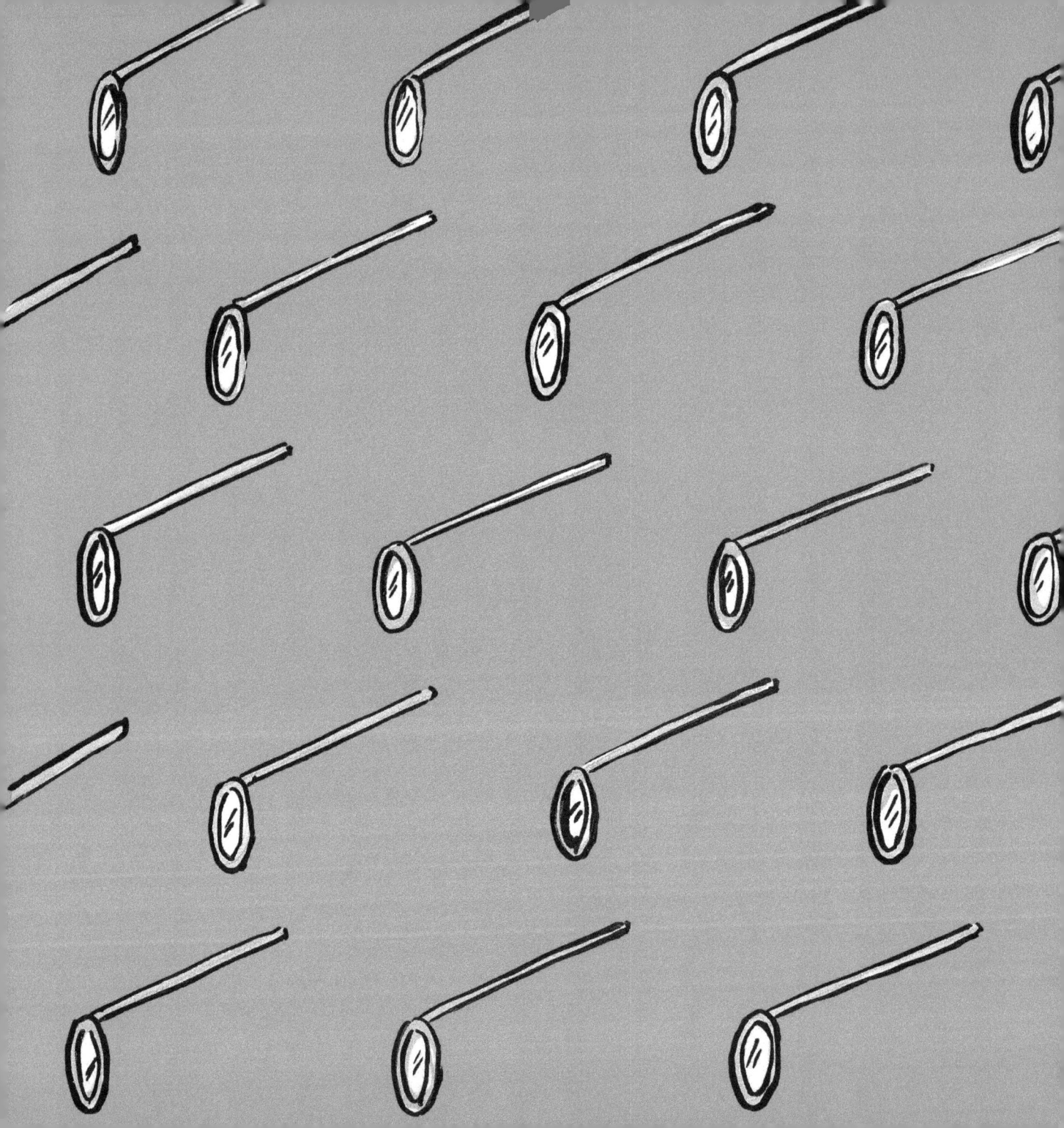

Dear Parents,

Children's earliest experiences with stories and books usually involve grown-ups reading to them. However, reading should be active, and as adults, we can help young readers make meaning of the text by prompting them to relate the book to what they already know and to their personal experiences. Our questions will lead them to move beyond the simple story and pictures and encourage them to think beneath the surface. For example, after reading a story about the sleep habits of animals, you might ask, "Do you remember when you moved into a big bed? Could you see the moon out of your window?"

Illustrations in these books are wonderful and can be used in a variety of ways. Your questions about them can direct the child to details and encourage him or her to think about what those details tell us about the story. You might ask the child to find three different "beds" used by animals and insects in the book. Illustrations can even be used to inspire readers to draw their own pictures related to the text.

At the end of each book, there are some suggested questions and activities related to the story. These questions range in difficulty and will help you move young readers from the text itself to thinking skills such as comparing and contrasting, predicting, applying what they learned to new situations and identifying things they want to find out more about. This conversation about their reading may even result in the children becoming the storytellers, rather than simply the listeners!

Harriet Ziefert, M.A.
Language Arts/Reading Specialist

More to  About

Does a Bear Wear Boots?

Does a Beaver Sleep in a Bed?

Does a Camel Cook Spaghetti?

Does a Hippo Go to the Doctor?

Does an Owl Wear Eyeglasses?

Does a Panda Go to School?

Does a Seal Smile?

Does a Woodpecker Use a Hammer?

 **how teeth stay healthy**

Does a Tiger Go to the Dentist?

Harriet Ziefert • illustrations by **Emily Bolam**

Text copyright © 2005, 2014 by Harriet Ziefert
Illustrations copyright © 2005 by Emily Bolam
All rights reserved
CIP data is available.
Published in the United States 2014 by
 Blue Apple Books
South Orange, New Jersey
www.blueapplebooks.com

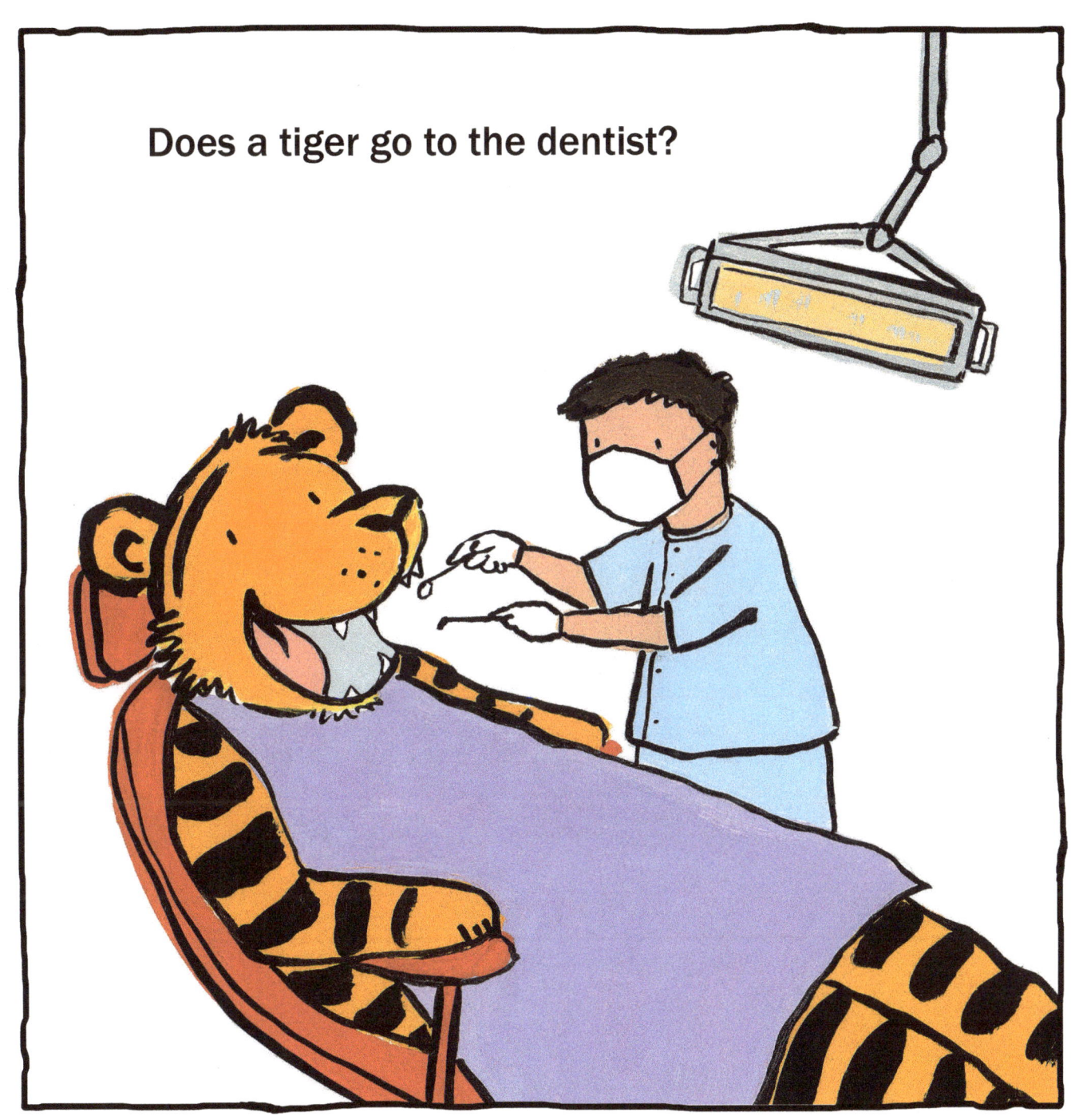

Oh, no!
A tiger would not sit in a dentist's chair.

Surely not!
A baboon would not allow the dentist
to put instruments in his mouth.

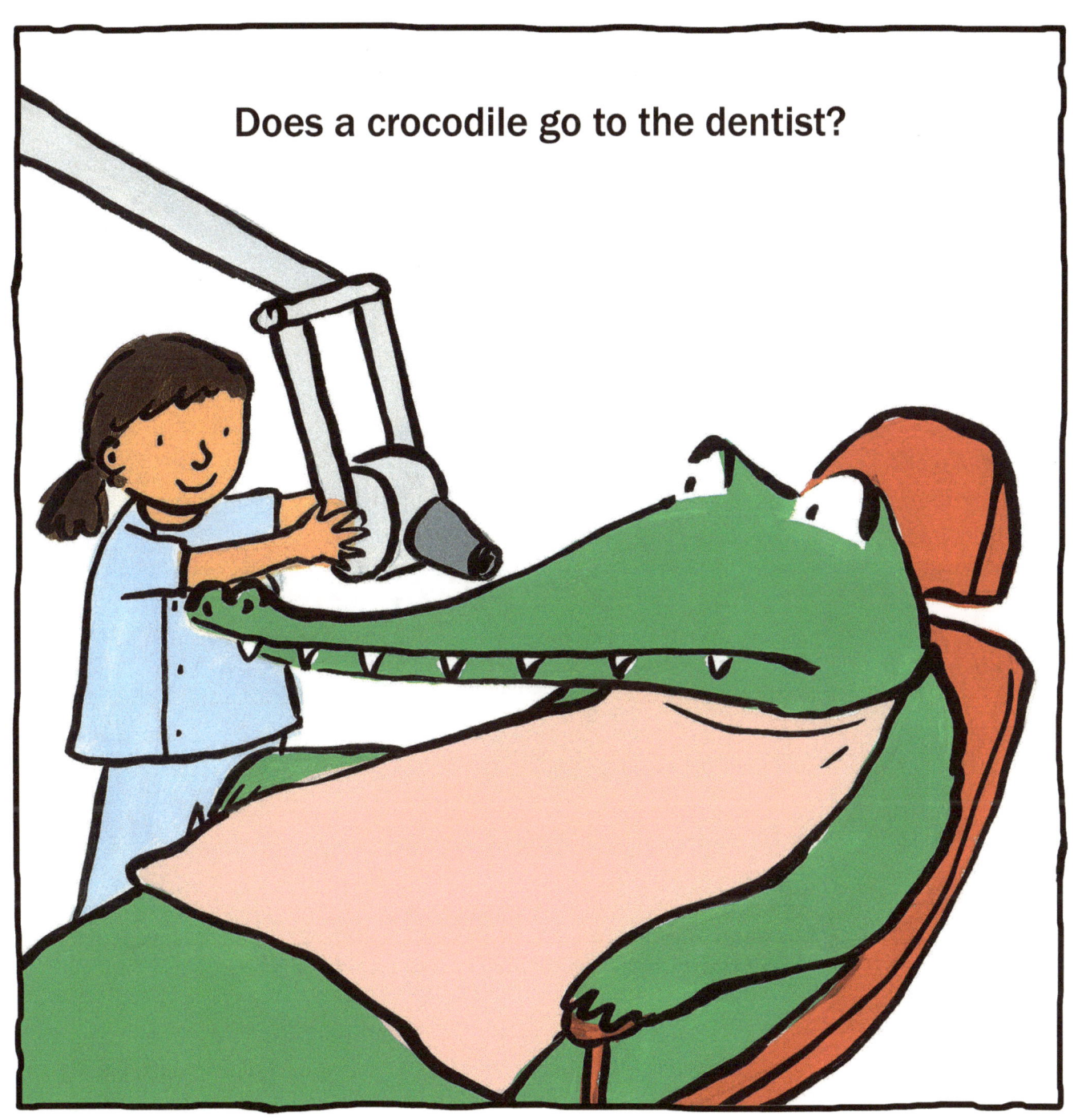

Never!
A crocodile would never permit
the dentist to take pictures of his teeth.

Does a wolf go to the dentist to get his teeth cleaned?

No, no!
A wolf would not allow a cleaning of his teeth. A wolf's teeth get cleaned by chewing and gnawing.

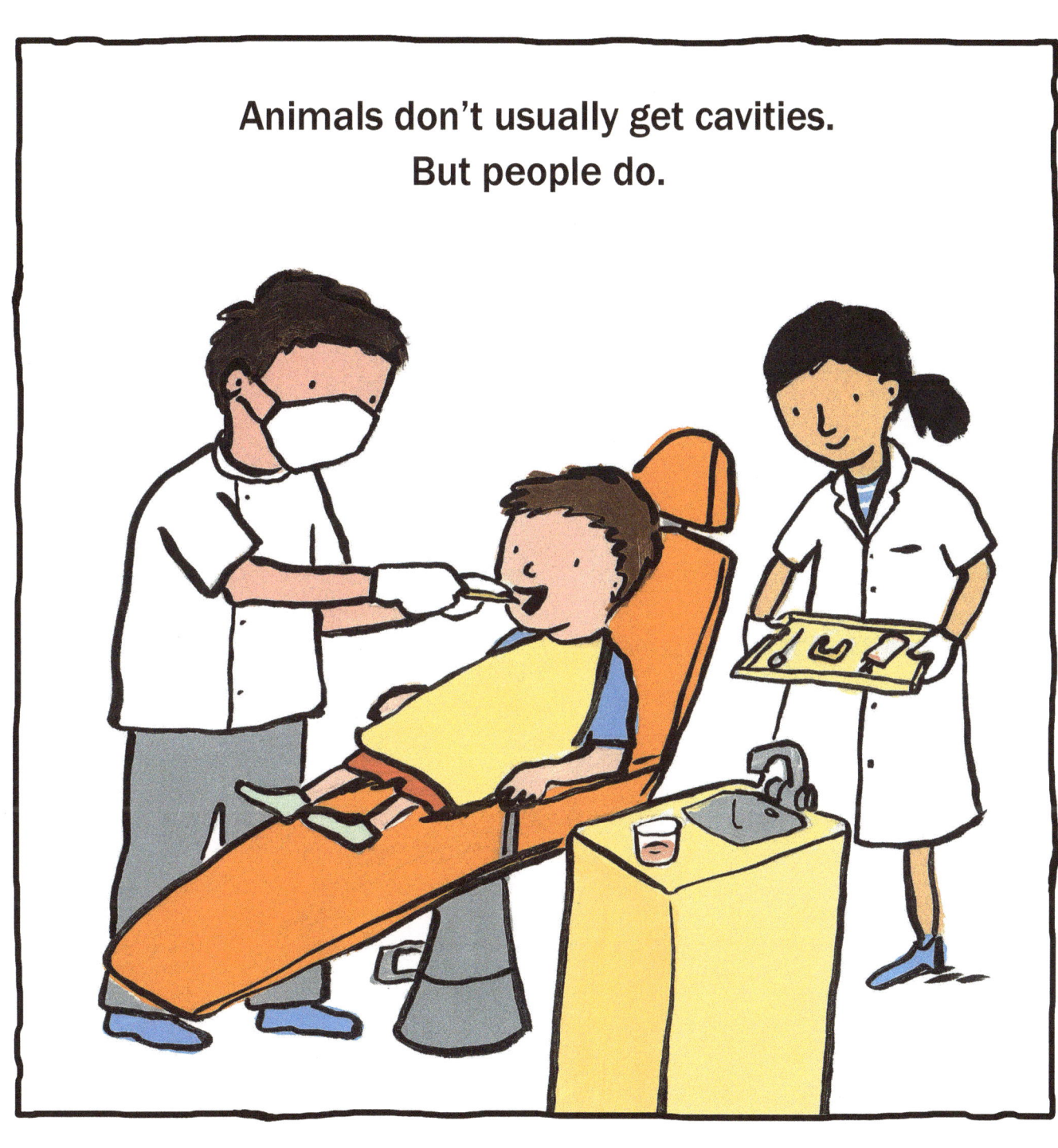

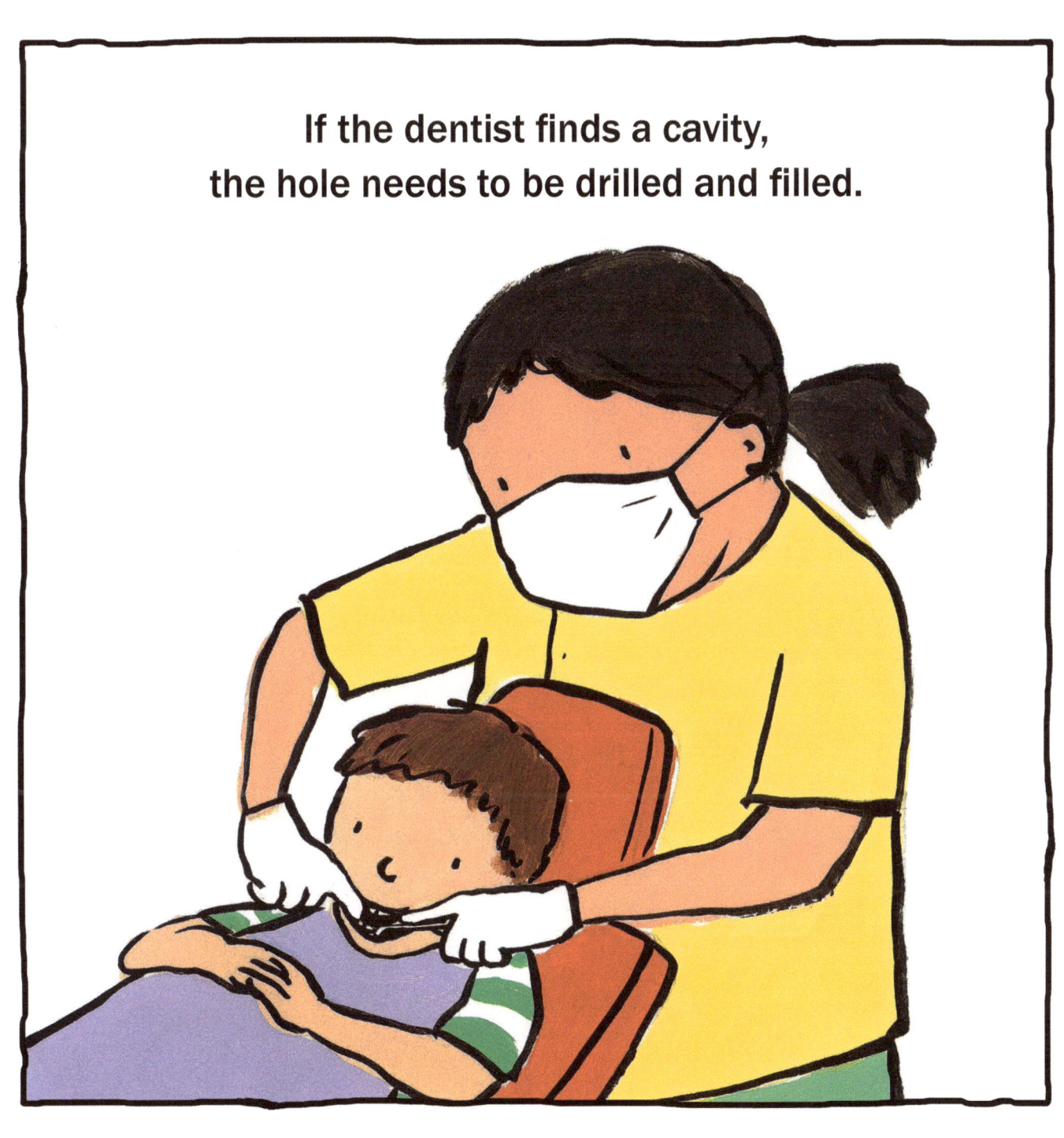

Mommies go to the dentist.
Daddies go.

Big kids go.
Little kids go.

Emily is not afraid of the dentist.
She knows what's going to happen
at the office.

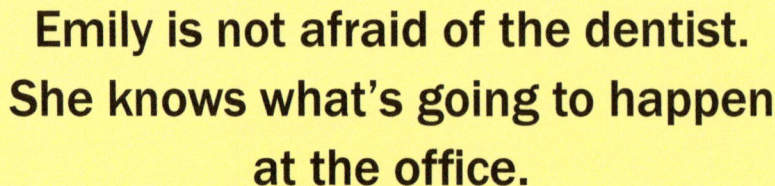

Dr. Dan says people should take care of their teeth with regular checkups.

Steps in a checkup:

1. dentist examines teeth with explorer and mirror

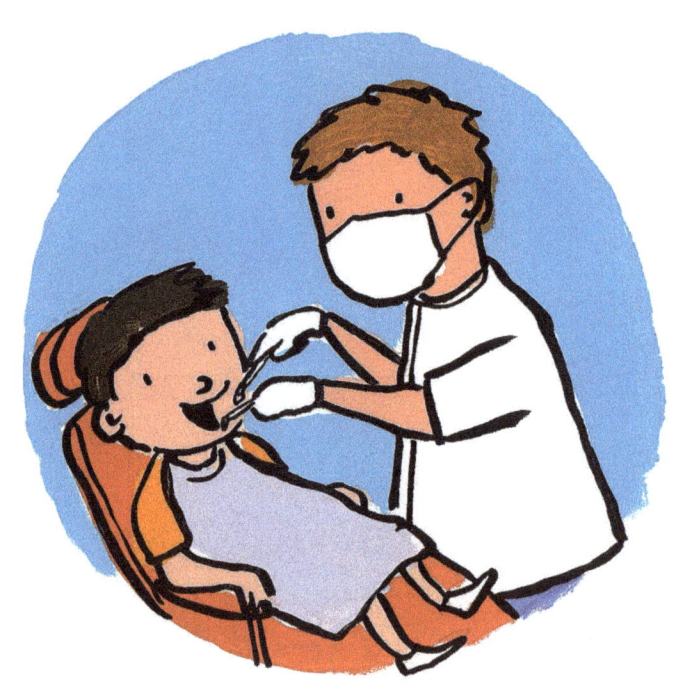

2. dentist x-rays teeth

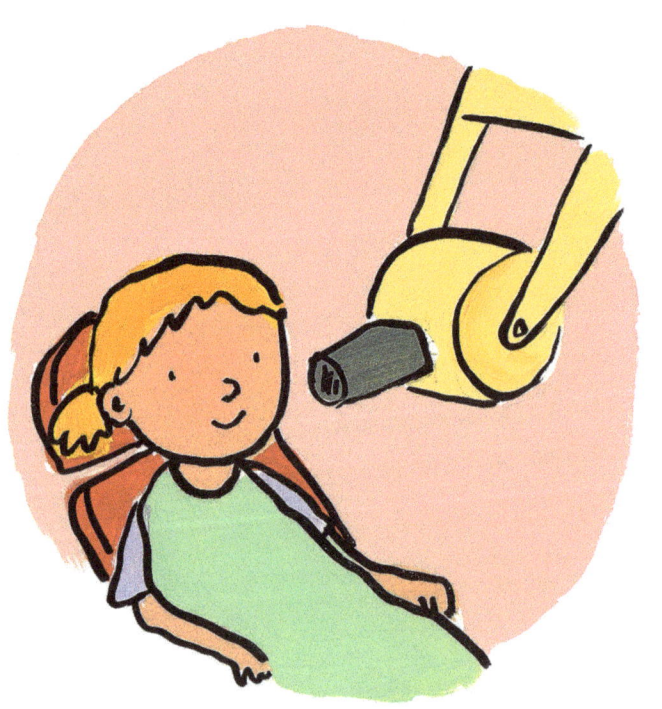

3. dentist cleans and polishes teeth

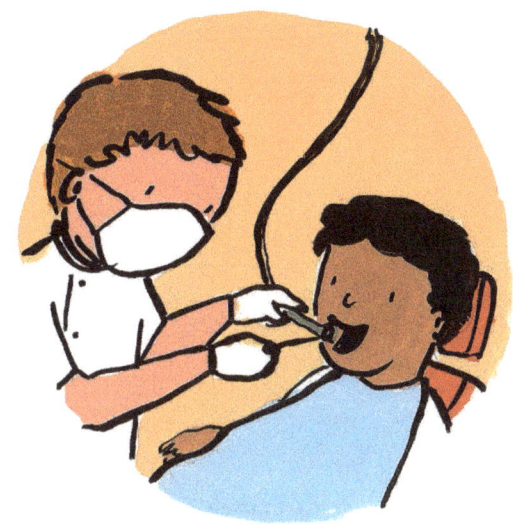

4. dentist gives fluoride treatment

5. dentist explains how to take care of your teeth

Nora brushes her teeth
at least twice every day.

Do you?

Think  About how teeth stay healthy

This book compares animals, which don't go to the dentist, with people, who need regular dental visits to keep their teeth clean and healthy.

Compare and Contrast

Inside your mouth you have different types of teeth.

- Compare and contrast the sizes and shapes of your teeth.
  Run your fingers over your teeth. Use a mirror.

- Compare biting a carrot to chewing a carrot.
  Do you use different teeth for each? Which takes longer? Chewing or biting?

- How does a wolf clean his teeth? How does a dog clean his teeth?
  How do you clean your teeth? Are there differences?

Research

Go to a library or online and find out:

- Were you born with teeth, or did your teeth come later?
  When did you get your first tooth?

- Find out why sugar is bad for your teeth.

- How many teeth do you have now?
  How many will you have when you're a grown-up?

Observe

- Try talking with your teeth closed. How do your words sound?
- Look at your teeth and your gums closely. Part of your tooth is hidden inside your gums. Can you see or feel the shape of the tooth underneath?

Write, Tell, or Draw

- Create a menu of all your favorite foods with words and pictures. Put a star next to the foods that you think your dentist would like you to eat.
- Ask someone in your family about your first tooth. Draw yourself as a baby smiling with just one tooth!
- Show step-by-step how you brush your teeth. Use words and pictures.
- Draw and label a picture of a tooth.

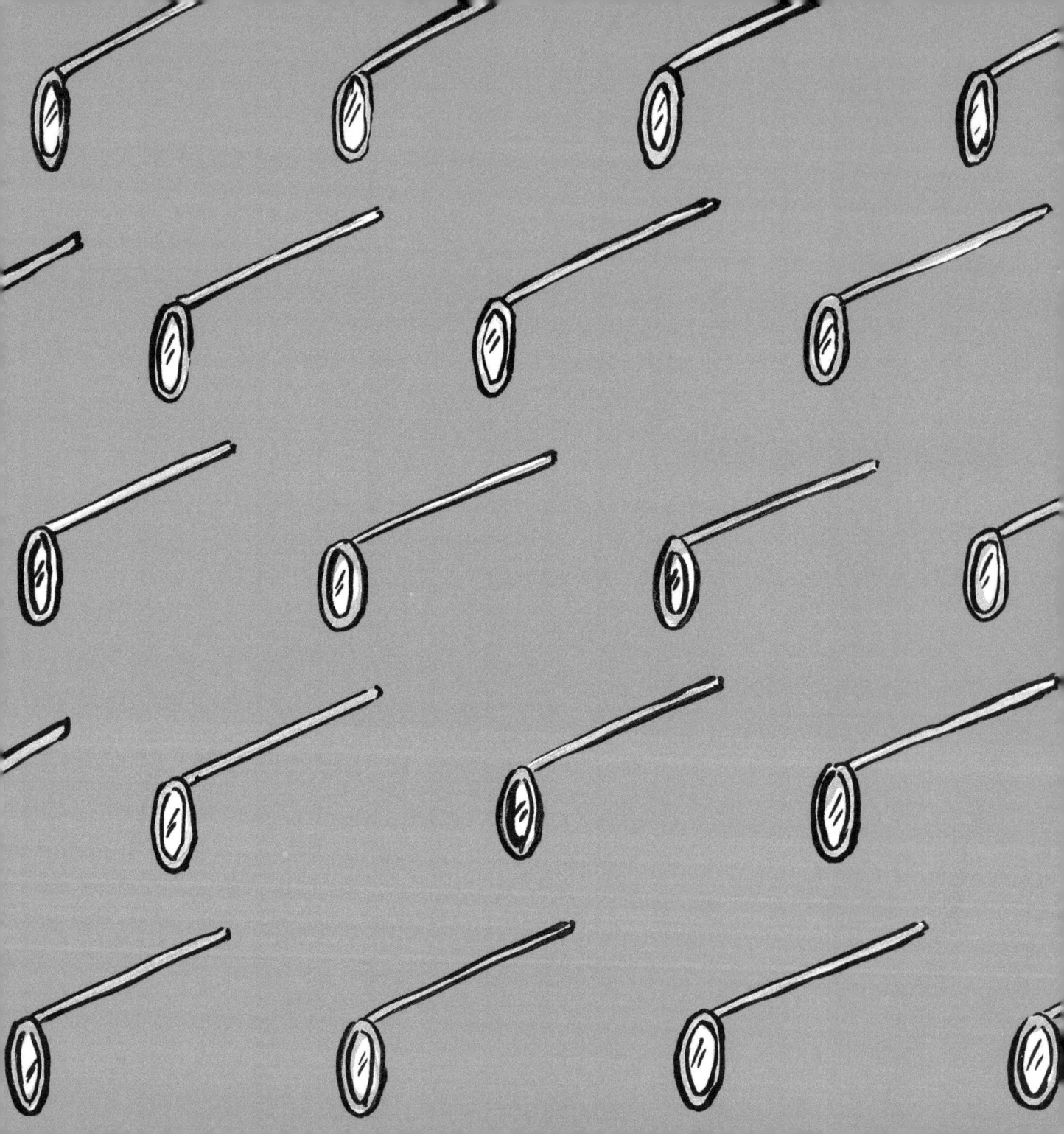